Look and Learn

A First Book about

Mixing and Matching

The original publishers would like to thank the following
children for modeling for this book: Daisy Bartlett,
April Cain, Jamie Grant, and Jack Harvey-Holt.

For a free color catalog describing Gareth Stevens
Publishing's list of high-quality books and multimedia
programs, call 1-800-542-2595 (USA) or 1-800-461-9120
(Canada). Gareth Stevens Publishing's Fax: (414) 225-0377.

Library of Congress Cataloging-in-Publication Data

Tuxworth, Nicola.
  A first book about mixing and matching / by Nicola Tuxworth.
    p. cm. — (Look and learn)
  Includes bibliographical references and index.
  Summary: Asks the reader to sort objects into different groups,
such as same colors, like shapes, and similar patterns or sizes.
    ISBN 0-8368-2371-0 (lib. bdg.)
  1. Set theory—Juvenile literature. [1. Set theory.] I. Title.
  II. Series: Tuxworth, Nicola. Look and learn.
  QA248.T88 1999
  511.3'22—dc21   98-31777

This North American edition first published in 1999 by
Gareth Stevens Publishing
1555 North RiverCenter Drive, Suite 201
Milwaukee, WI 53212 USA

Original edition © 1997 by Anness Publishing Limited.
First published in 1997 by Lorenz Books, an imprint
of Anness Publishing Inc., New York, New York.
This U.S. edition © 1999 by Gareth Stevens, Inc.
Additional end matter © 1999 by Gareth Stevens, Inc.

Editor: Sophie Warne
Photographer: John Freeman
Stylist: Isolde Sommerfeldt
Design and typesetting: Liz Black

Printed in Mexico

1 2 3 4 5 6 7 8 9 03 02 01 00 99

Look and Learn

A First Book about

Mixing and Matching

Nicola Tuxworth

Gareth Stevens Publishing
MILWAUKEE

Pairs

Two matching
shoes make
a pair.

pair of shoes

Can you find all
the pairs?

How many pairs
of shoes are there?

5

Colors

Objects come in different colors.

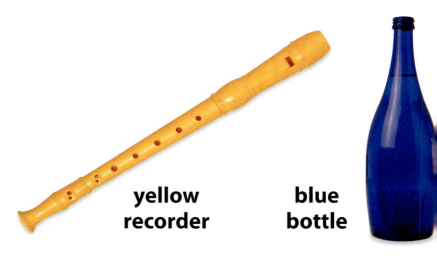

yellow recorder

blue bottle

Can you sort these objects by color?

brown pinecone

green apple

red crayon

How many green objects can you find?

Patterns

Some objects come in different patterns.

checked socks

Can you sort these objects by pattern?

8

polka-dotted balloon

striped pencil

Do *you* have anything that is striped?

Shapes

Objects come in different shapes.

Can you sort these objects by shape?

triangular napkin

round plate

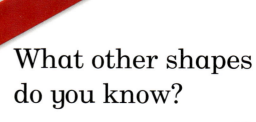

What other shapes
do you know?

Sizes

Objects come in different sizes.

smallest

Can you put the ducks, dolls, and boxes in order by size?

12

biggest

Who is the smallest
in your family?

Partners

A paddle and ball
are partners.

ball

paddle

Can you find the partners
on these pages?

Can you think of
any other partners?

Dressing up

The cowboy needs a hat to complete his outfit.

cowboy hat

cowboy

What do the pirate, ballerina, and clown need?

What would you
like to dress up as?

Are there enough?

There are enough cherries for the cupcakes.

cherries

Do the kittens have a saucer of milk each?

cupcakes

Are there enough spoons for the ice-cream sundaes?

Clothes

You need to wear different clothes for different kinds of weather.

What does Jane need to wear in the sunshine?

What does Jack
need to wear
in the cold?

Sort it out!

Can you sort
these objects?

Can you find
a pair of socks?

How many
polka-dotted
objects are there?

How many blue
objects do you see?

Can you find
the clown's hat
and nose?

Glossary/Index

matching (*v*): grouping similar or identical objects together. (p. 4)

mixing: putting objects together.

order: an arrangement of objects, one after another. (p. 12)

outfit: various pieces of clothing that are worn together as a unit. (p. 16)

pair: a set of two objects that are alike or that belong together. (pp. 4, 5, 22)

partners: objects that belong together. (pp. 14, 15)

patterns: designs — such as zigzag lines, circles, or stripes — on an item. (p. 8)

recorder: a type of flute. (p. 6)

sort: to separate objects into groups so all the objects in each group are alike or follow a pattern. (pp. 6, 8, 10, 22)

More Books to Read

Dots, Spots, Speckles, and Stripes. Tana Hoban (Greenwillow Books)

Little Mouse's Learn-and-Play (series). Anaël Dena (Gareth Stevens)

Science Buzzwords (series). Karen Bryant-Mole (Gareth Stevens)

Shapes. Anne Geddes (Cedco)

Videos

Blue's Clues Shape Detective. (Viacom International)

Colors & Shapes. (Good Times Home Video)

Web Sites

www.wildlifeportraits.com/zebra.htm

www.funschool.com/

Some web sites stay current longer than others. For further web sites, use your search engines to locate the following topics: *colors, patterns, shapes,* and *sorting*.